# Verses that mean a lot

'Growing up'

# Books in the series

## For young people

'Growing up'
'Coping with Illness and Grief'
'Choice for Teenagers'

## For adults

Several volumes of therapeutic poems – in preparation

# Verses that mean a lot

## 'Growing up'

by
Dr Audrey Coatesworth

Published by PLP Publishings, Buckingham, March 2007

NOTE to the READER
This publication does not attempt to dispense or prescribe for or treat medical or psychological problems. If the reader - or other for whom this publication is intended, has significant difficulties in life it is highly recommended that they seek an appropriate health practitioner.

Printed and bound by Moreton Press, Buckingham

## Ordering information

**Tel/answerphone:** 01280 823401
**Website:** www.plppublishings.co.uk

# Acknowledgements

## Grateful thanks to:-

Peter – for unstinting devotion and love

Catherine – for endless patience and care

David – for illustrating selected poems

Wayne and Brian – for their expertise and courage in saving my life

Toby and Ella – for reading the poems and for their comments

Melanie – for her constructive interest and enthusiasm

Brian and Nick – for invaluable help in the preparation of the books

The original pictures were all painted by
Yorkshire artist **David S Earnshaw**

# Introduction - for adults to read

I trained at Edinburgh University Medical School and qualified as a Doctor in 1962. After my children started school and for the next thirty five years, until my recent retirement, I worked as a psychiatrist. I worked part time to fit in with school hours- against the tide or prejudice for women.

My psychiatric training was made possible by the insight and vision of one remarkable woman - Dr Rosemary Rue. She created the part-time women's training scheme in the Oxford Region - recognising the needs of both the married women doctors and their children.

As a Consultant, most of my time was spent treating the unresolved traumas, recent and past, of those patients who came into my care. The resulting negative memories and connected beliefs, consciously or unconsciously stored in the mind, caused many of the emotional problems both for the patient and within their interpersonal relationships.

Many traumas dated back to events in childhood - deliberate, accidental or unfortunate. The effects were not only causing great distress many years later but, in more general terms, had very limiting consequences for the adult. Children who are unhappy or hurt should be able to release the emotion so the event can heal, and be given and be able to receive comfort and understanding. All children are different in their reactions.

Life is eventful. Trauma, illness and grief can not be avoided and successfully overcoming adversity, big or small, is an essential part of emotional growth. But prevention of trauma, sudden or prolonged, if and when possible,is still the best strategy.

My belief, as a mother and grandmother, but subsequently strengthened through my work, is that the safe and loving care of children is the greatest responsibility that anyone can undertake. There is no adequate substitute for a parent or close family member in the first few years. That care is not only for the 'present' but for the 'future' of the child. As much time and effort as is possible should be freely given once parenthood is chosen or accepted.

It is my belief that time that is missed cannot be regained for child or parent - however important other aspects of life may appear at the time. Long lasting love, understanding, happiness or respect can never be bought - and the available years are but short.

I write this and my verses to let another voice be heard on behalf of our children. As a psychiatrist I feel both worried and sad about what is happening to so many children at this present time.

My own earliest years (2-9 yrs) were during the anxious and 'deprived' days of the Second World War – 'deprived' in the sense of the lack of material possessions of the modern day child.

For me, the most deprived aspect of my childhood was the absence of effective medication and thus I had to live and cope with chronic ill health in the form of severe asthma and chest infections. Thermogene pads on the chest, hot kaolin poultices, a linctus – all my dad's favourite 'a drop of medicinal rum and honey' – did nothing to stop the devastation of body and spirit. Neither had they the power to fight the infections.

This was a time when scarlet fever needed several weeks in an isolation hospital and friends and school mates died or were maimed as a result of polio. A mother had little to use to help her child - except give constant care and time.

The inspiration for my verses has come from several sources – my own childhood, my children's childhoods, the sayings and behaviour of my grandchildren, from other children I have known or observed and from my many years of work.

The verses in this volume are intended for any young person from about 8-9 yrs upwards, happy or not, well or ill.  I hope they will be read by young people, but also to them by their parents, grandparents, teachers and all those privileged to work with and care for children. I can also read to them via the CDs I have made for each book.

I would prefer that young people find their own meaning in the verses and do not have them explained. However, because of the wide range of age and ability some words may need to be explained. Many are written as 'stories' and all are deliberately written in verse with a gentle message.

My aim is to try to help today's children (and maybe their parents) understand that life is not easy - whether privileged or poor. Neither is it about having the most material possessions, but about kindness, enthusiasm, courage, determination, effort and hope. Happiness and fulfilment come from within.

My title was going to be 'Learning through Life', but then I asked my granddaughter, aged eleven – after she read the verses – what did she think? After a while she said, 'Verses that mean a lot '. Hence the title of the series.

My eldest brother, David S Earnshaw, a retired timber merchant, has illustrated those of my verses which were suitable for illustration. I hope you enjoy his delightful pictures, done originally in water colours. He wanted to paint, I wanted to write. For us, these were not options as a way of life. Now, in our retirement years, they are!

The verses are dedicated to the beloved children in my life, but are written on behalf of children everywhere.

I have written many other poems for young people in books 'Choice for Teenagers' and 'Coping with Illness and Grief'. The adult books are in preparation.

I hope my verses - in books and on CDs – continue my therapeutic work within this different medium.

On behalf of myself and my brother David S Earnshaw who gave me the illustrations, I shall donate £1 from the sale of every one of my three children's poetry books in this series **'Verses that mean a lot' – 'Growing up', 'Coping with Illness and Grief' and 'Choices for Teenagers'** to selected children's charities as/when via PLP Publishings.

Dr Audrey Coatesworth
March, 2007

# CONTENTS

| | | | |
|---|---|---|---|
| Judge Me Not | 1 | A Bird | 59 |
| Letter to Mrs Mouse | 3 | Daydreams | 60 |
| A Perfect World | 4 | Friends | 61 |
| Choosing A Name | 5 | A Pain | 63 |
| Playing In The Sand | 7 | Bullied | 64 |
| Puzzles | 8 | Alarm Clock | 65 |
| Distance | 9 | The Pear Tree | 67 |
| The Dolls House | 11 | Patience And Courage | 68 |
| Dreams | 12 | At The End Of The Day | 69 |
| A Holiday | 13 | Nature | 71 |
| A Lesson In Obedience | 15 | Soon | 72 |
| What's In A Name | 16 | Temper Tantrums | 73 |
| Goodnight | 17 | The Necklace | 75 |
| My Kitten | 19 | The Squirrels | 76 |
| If | 20 | What Am I Worth | 77 |
| Seabirds | 21 | The Acer | 79 |
| The Moth | 23 | Wishes | 80 |
| A Matter Of Opinion | 24 | Boredom | 81 |
| The Other Side | 25 | Seals | 83 |
| My Garden | 27 | Plans | 84 |
| Knowing Best | 28 | The Yellow Teaset | 85 |
| Choices | 29 | Harmony | 87 |
| The Oogly – Woogly Bird | 31 | The Wind | 88 |
| Once In A While | 32 | Boys And Girls | 89 |
| Normal Reaction | 33 | Grandma's Apples | 91 |
| Sunshine | 35 | The Copper Beech Tree | 92 |
| My Bike | 36 | School Trip To The Seaside | 93 |
| Trying Hard | 37 | Favourite Place | 95 |
| The Carousel | 39 | Going To Sleep | 96 |
| My Hobby | 40 | Goblins | 97 |
| My Horse | 41 | Cleaning The Attic | 99 |
| The Little Train | 43 | Contrast | 100 |
| Lost Opportunity | 44 | Clouds Of Love | 101 |
| Mummy's Message | 45 | Aunt Polly's Gift | 103 |
| The Rocking Horse | 47 | The Birth Day Cake | 104 |
| Mrs Squirrel | 48 | | |
| My Animals | 49 | | |
| Things That Cannot Be Bought | 51 | | |
| Imagination | 52 | | |
| Baking Day | 53 | | |
| Little Things | 55 | | |
| Playing A Game | 56 | | |
| Santa | 57 | | |

# Judge Me Not

Judge me not by my face
My colour or my hair
Judge me not by appearance
As that would not be fair
I came to earth as I am
No discussion of my look
I had no pattern to study
No choice from any book

Judge me not by ability
To read, write, or understand
Let it be by all my effort
The use put to my hand
The **courage** in bad times
**Endurance** getting through
**Kindness** to another

So please-

*Judge me by what I do*

# Letter To Mrs Mouse

Mrs Mouse could I request
You do not use my home
Please keep out of all my rooms
Where you're not free to roam

When you ran along the pipes
In my room the other night
I nearly fell out of bed
You gave me such a fright

I thought the cupboard was secure
But yet you made me jump
When I opened up the door
And I gave my head a bump

The apples in the larder
That I placed upon the shelf
Are not put there for you to eat
I want them for myself

Your habits quite disgust me
You smell and you're not clean
You may be called a field mouse
But I don't know where you've been

If you will stay out of doors
You can use the garden shed
In winter to keep you warm
And I will give you bread

I will not use a mouse trap
I could not hurt you like that
But if you don't heed my words

*I might just get a cat*

# A Perfect World

I looked out of my window
At the moon and stars above
I asked myself the question
What could be done by love?

Wars would cease and hunger
Would be ended as all spare grain
Would be shared with those in need
Without any thought of gain

No injuries caused by wicked hand
The reason – no longer found
Everyone would walk in peace
Upon earth's fragile ground

I see people of different races
Laughing in light so bright
Children playing, free from harm
Walking safely, day and night

But then I realise it is make-belief
I make a drink, go back to bed
I sleep till morning, awake to find
That world only in my head

Can you help change this world of ours?
Will you make a happier place?
How better than a world of tears
Would be a smile on every face

# Choosing A Name

What shall we call her?
Is Elizabeth quite right?
Or Susan or Tracey?
Oh, don't let us fight
I can't imagine a Mary
When I see her face
But Georgina or Jane
Just seem out of place
Kate or Rebecca?
We've said those before
Charlotte or Jennifer?
There must be some more
Through the Alphabet
From A to Z
Names are just buzzing
All round in my head
If we don't get it right
She may complain
When she gets older
And not like her name
Such a difficult task
I never did know
We could pick from a hat
And any name show
We can not ask her
What she would choose
Such a responsibility
We could win or could lose
Maria, Audrey, Rose
Betty, Ella, Daisy May?
Oh, let's call her 'darling'
For just one more day

# Playing In The Sand

A lovely way to spend a day is playing with some sand
Building castles with a spade, a bucket near at hand
You may need to fetch some water if your castle will not set
Dry sand will just spill out, yes, it really must be wet

If you are playing on a beach, dig where the sea has been
The sand will be just perfect, you'll soon see what I mean
You can make one big one and many small as well
Decorate with twigs and stones, put on the top a shell

You may be adventurous, make a car or dig a boat
Or just be quite happy with a castle, walls and moat
Playing in the sand and protected from the sun
Is relaxing, it's creative, but most of all, it's fun

Now:-

On the beach, most would say, that children seldom fight
Playing together easily from morning until night
What a lesson to be learned, by all, for every day
Something is different – why should it be this way?

*– I wonder-does anybody know?*

# Puzzles

'On the other side of the world
When all is upside down
Can you sit on normal chairs?'
The girl asked with a frown

'Must you sleep on wet sand
So you do not fall at night?'
She asked again to clarify
She could not see it right

'I can hear you very clearly
On the phone, how can that be?
There are no wires over the sea
Can you explain it all to me?'

'Where did the light go I wonder?
Has it gone out through the wall?
Mummy has switched the switch
And I can't see at all'

'Were you born very clever?
To know so many things
Or did you learn to be so?
Is that what studying brings?'

'Shall I ever know the answers
To endless questions in my mind?'

*'One day you will understand*
*Just now you are a child*
*Exercise* **curiosity** *every day*
*Let* **enthusiasm** *be well fed*
*Then you will learn and soon know how*
*To sort puzzles in your head'*

# **Distance**

If I cannot see and I cannot show
My love for you, will you still know?

A birthday remembered, a letter sent
Will you notice what the message meant?

If I must play just a little part
Can you feel what is in my heart

Only by phone do you hear my voice
In many things we have no choice

What is the answer to distance long?
Can we have a bond that's strong?

I do not know the answer clear
Just understand, you are always dear

Time and place will change one day
Then all our sadness will fly away

# The Doll's House

My doll's house is beautiful, I have made it out of wood
Painted with clear varnish, it's almost ready and it looks good
The kitchen needs crockery, the bedroom – blankets blue
The lounge – two arm chairs, so, a few things still to do

The balcony will be sunny and warm on a summer's day
Light and airy rooms are just perfect for dolls to play
An open porch has three steps, so they can sit and rest
The roof will be quite waterproof, yes, it really is the best

∞

I used to see a doll's house – when I was only small
I seldom got to play with it, as I needed to be tall
I wanted to touch, but someone kept it on a shelf
My fingers wouldn't reach, I couldn't manage by myself

It was rarely lifted down, but no one told me why
I just gazed longingly – then would often start to cry
I remember it had chairs with cushions of purple satin
The bed had a pillowcase with a white, fine lacy pattern

∞

The lesson it taught me I have remembered all my years

**Never want what isn't yours**
**Or the day may end in tears**

**BUT**

*'I have made mine – just for you, and the work will be worthwhile*
*If when you are all playing, I can see it makes you smile'*

# Dreams

**1.**
'When will my dream come true
And I wear a ring of gold?'
'When the Magnolia blossoms'
The little girl was told

**2.**
'Will I ever reach the stars
And swing on sunbeams warm?'
'When the Magnolia blossoms
Then you'll be safe from harm'

**3.**
'When will my pain disappear
So I can swim and run?'
'When the Magnolia blossoms
Then you will have some fun'

**4.**
'When does the Magnolia blossom?'
The little girl asked in vain
'When new Spring comes around
And you can smile again'

**5.**
'When will that ever happen?
It's dark, it seems so late'
'When the Magnolia blossoms
Till then you have to wait'

**6.**
'Please, somebody tell me when?'
Was her mournful cry
'When the Magnolia blossoms
You'll get there if you try'

**7.**
She finally accepted fate
But her dreams she still held dear
'When the Magnolia blossoms
It will bloom for you one year'

**8.**
'Which year?'. She did not give up
Her quest the truth to know
'When the Magnolia blossoms
To your eyes the flowers will show'

**9.**
'What if frost comes that year
And the flowers are all destroyed?'
'The Magnolia again will blossom'
Earth's cycle will be employed'

**10.**
'So I must just carry on and on
And with everything just cope?'
'The Magnolia tree will blossom
Each year will bring new hope'

12

# A Holiday

Being by the seaside
Can mean holidays in the sun
Paddling at the water's edge
Having lots of fun

Breezes blowing thin and chill
Walking in the rain
Disappointing weather
Cold and wet again

Catching shrimps in rock pools
Fishing from the pier
Being tired and hungry with
Sand in shoes and hair

Icecream in crisp cornet
Picnics on the ground
Waking every morning to the
Seagulls' screeching sound

Something to wait all year for
Bucket and spade at hand
Best of all, without a doubt
Is building castles in the sand

No need for noisy music
No need for fancy toys
Sea and sand - in rain or shine
Make happy girls and boys

# A Lesson In Obedience

We were having a picnic in a beauty spot, well known
We had been there many times, it felt almost like our own
We were all quite young and we always had good fun
A tree had lovely branches -on them we climbed and swung
The stream was very shallow, our wellingtons were great
As we could paddle, lift small stones, and a dam create
We were busy with our game, when suddenly we heard
A roar behind us. What was that? We knew it wasn't a bird
Our mums shouted loudly 'Leave everything NOW and run'
We raced to the gate, and **immediately** left our fun

We all climbed quickly over the bars, we really had no choice
As the bull came charging at us, it made a dreadful noise
It's rope had torn, it got away, and the farmer hadn't seen
But it was very dangerous, it looked wild and very mean
We all thought that we were safe, you really cannot know
What will happen in your life as through each day you go
Our mums took us to play and they were always very kind
So if we had to stop our game, we tried hard not to mind
But, we were only safe then as we did what we were told
Yes, our Mums knew best -they are wiser - they are old


They were so pleased and hugged us and said how good we were

**But**

With the farmer they were angry and

(**sshh ─── I will whisper this**)

'we **actually** heard them swear'

# What's In A Name?

'My name doesn't fit'

*The young girl said*

'It isn't the name
I have in my head

How did you know
This one to give?
That I must use
As long as I live

What made you choose
This name for me?
It isn't mine
Couldn't you see?

I must keep it
Wear it with pride
Show I am me
From deep inside

Then it won't matter
What is my name
As I am still me
I am just the same'

# __Goodnight__

Usually, I go to sleep at night in my lovely bed, all warm
I snuggle down and very soon another day will dawn
Sometimes, though, I don't sleep because I don't feel right
I keep everyone awake, so no one sleeps all night

The next day they ask. 'Why should I treat them so?'
'I am not being fair,' they say 'I'm old enough to know'
I just want some attention, but no one tells me why
I know I get most everything. Why do I need to cry?

I sometimes make a fuss, when on and on I go
I don't stop, I really don't, once I start it seems to grow
They say it is time to understand I must not be this way
I should lie down in my bed and sleep until next day

**They say:-**

I really have to tell myself I am not a baby now
Older children should sleep well without a fuss or row
I should think of nice things, of people who love me
Feel happy and be content,  so, that is how I'll try to be

**Then they say:-**

I should go straight to sleep, wake with the morning light
They must go to their work, need to wake up feeling bright

'Oh dear, I have been silly and given them such a plight

**I hope that what they say is right**
                              **and that it works for me tonight'**

17

# My Kitten

I used to have a kitten but I haven't, I don't know how
I lost it. Can you help me to try and find it now?
Has anyone seen a kitten? It should be somewhere near
It is ginger coloured with a white stripe by its ear

It has the sweetest little face, its eyes are very blue
If you happen to see it, you will love it too
It is only very tiny, as it isn't very old
It is too young to wander - but can't do what it's told

It is not where I left it, in a basket in the barn
I want it to come back to where it was safe and warm
It had lots of milk to drink and a lovely soft warm bed
It lived with two other cats and a happy life it led

Please don't let it get hurt, where ever it may be
No rat or fox to find it, no nasty dog to see
I thought I saw it yesterday, and I called its name
But when I went to look, that kitten was not the same

'Please come back little kitten, you do not need to stray
I shall keep on looking for you – every single day
I only want you to be safe, and loved as you should be
By someone kind and gentle'


**Oh - how I wish it was still me**

# **<u>If</u>**

If I can count right up to four
Why can't I open any door?

If a straight line has no bend
Why do I not reach the end?

If stairs lead up and also down
Why do I always see a frown?

If the sun hides behind a cloud
Does it hear me shout quite loud?

If you travel to a far off land
Must you sleep on rock or sand?

If the world is the same at night
Why is it different without a light?

If I grow old to nine or ten
Will I be allowed to use a pen?

If every day follows every day
How does anything ever stay?

If I ask questions all the time
I shall not hear the big clock chime

If I get lost in all my thinking
The day is gone, the sun is sinking

If I can learn another way
Maybe I'll understand one day

# Seabirds

I am a heron, I live by the sea
Alone, I stand on the rock
I catch fish and I just watch
I have no need of any flock

A gannet, with black tipped wings
I am graceful, full of poise
High dives never hurt my head
I catch fish without a noise

An oyster catcher, always busy
My leggings are red and neat
I race around with my friends
At the water's edge we meet

A shag, racing back and forth
No part of a day I waste
With little time to dive or fish
I do everything in haste

A seagull, raucous, shouting  loud
Stealing food beneath your nose
Idly waits, then makes a mess

**I will not be one of those**

# The Moth

The little moth went to look
For food in wardrobe near
It saw the jackets hanging there
Blue, pink and black, oh dear
'I will have a feast' it said
'This must be my lucky day
I'll eat as much as possible
And then I'll just fly away'

First, it tried the blue one
Tiny holes made at the back
It didn't taste very nice
So it moved on to the black
It kept the pink for pudding
Had a very good meal, I'd say
Made many holes that in despair
The coat was thrown away

I would give the moth a T-shirt
If I thought it could understand
But it just flies anywhere
Eats whatever is to hand
Now I am telling you all this
But to the moth I can't explain
As I do not think that you will find
A moth has got a brain

I believe and you may not
With my opinion agree
But if I work very hard
My things **should** belong to me
I think those who spoil or steal
Must have brains all in a bundle
They behave no better than a moth
They should go live in a jungle

# A Matter Of Opinion

'This garden is full of many things
Now listen while I talk'
'What do you observe' the teacher asked
'As we go on this nice walk?'

'I see fruit trees and flowering shrubs'
'Delphiniums by the score'
'I see the roses blooming'
'And the topiary by that door'

'The many different shades of green'
'The water lilies in the pond'
'I see the bushes of lavender
Of which grandma was so fond'

'What do you see', she asked a child
'As we walk around the place?'
He was taking little notice
'Look this way, so I see your face'

'I don't know the names of any
We haven't got a garden'
Then some children began to laugh
Without a word of pardon

As they were walking one girl fell
She tripped against a fence
'Do watch where you're going
Just learn a bit of sense'

The little boy with no garden
Bent down to help the girl
He may not have known any names
But in his heart was a hidden pearl

He did not shine in the classroom
Nor do maths, or knowledge learn
Some things, not learned from a book
The highest mark should earn

# The Other Side

I think I have had the flu
Said the spider to the fly
My legs feel like jelly
And I just want to cry
I cannot spin
I cannot run
I tell you this
Life isn't much fun

I'm sorry you are feeling ill
But for me that fact is good
Or else I wouldn't be talking
You'd eat me as your food
I can fly
And I can dance
Your illness gives me
Another chance

# My Garden

Where shall I put the shingle?
Where the flags on which to tread?
What shall I choose to plant?
To create the picture in my head
I want to make the garden
A place to sit and rest
Where ever then I cast my eyes
That part will look the best

Not a lot of work is wanted
But tranquillity and peace
Not backbreaking digging
But a place to feel at ease
I love to see some bright blooms
And smell a fragrance sweet
But there may not be any room
To grow anything good to eat

A chair and bench for sitting
A table for tea and cake
A swinging seat for sleeping
A real oasis I will make
The blackbird and red robin
Can share the space with me
I think I can hear them say
'It's a grand place for us to be'

We all need peace and quiet
In our busy bustling lives
If anyone looked from above
They would think we needed hives
Like bees we travel here and there
With purpose – or without
But everyone needs somewhere
That never hears a shout

# Knowing Best

I do not want to go to bed
I 'm going to climb that tree
I want to watch the telly
I am a big girl, can't you see?
I want to wear my summer top
I am very warm, not cold
The snow does not hurt me
I can decide now I am old
I will not wear those horrid shoes
Nowhere would I dare to go
Blue and green, yellow and red
I like colour, you should know
My hair is fine, I like it long
Do not hurt me when you brush
I cannot get ready faster
I can't find things if I rush

**Oh dear – do I see tears??**

Can you help me? I have a bruise
I fell off the branch – though low
I think a cold is coming on and
My streaming nose must blow
I wish my shoes were stronger
The stones all hurt my feet
I cannot sleep, I'm hungry
And my homework isn't neat
I tripped over all my clothes
At school someone pulled my hair
I haven't done my reading
Oh, life just isn't fair

'I am sorry, I will listen
Yes, what you said was right

And — Mummy — I do love you
Please would you hug me?

**Really tight'**

# Choices

Did you decide your birthday?
Who you were going to be?
Did you choose your family?
Or what place you would see
When you opened up your eyes
Soon after you were born?
Which country you would live in?
Some places are so forlorn

No choice

Did you decide the colour
That both your eyes would be?
Your teeth,your hair and stature?
That would be news to me.
To have brothers and sisters?
Or never to have any
To be well and strong or weak?
These questions are so many

No choice

Do you decide how to behave?
What to say and how to cope?
For some it is just very hard
To live life without hope
So sad that some are very ill
And miss out on life's fun
But sadder still to waste the gifts
By getting nothing done

Some choice

To be nasty or show jealousy?
Or our precious time just waste?
To destroy health by habits?
To behave with undue haste?
To not value what we were given?
To not look amidst the dross
For the jewels of our existence
Until the final bridge we cross?

We all have choice

# The Oogly - Woogly Bird

'I'll make an Oogly - Woogly bird'
The little girl told her mother
'Will you help me to do it?
And look after my little brother
So he doesn't pull it all apart?'
*'Of course'* was her mum's reply
*'But I haven't heard of such a bird*
*Do you think that it will fly?'*

'We need coloured paper, feathers
Paints and glue, then I can show
Mummy, I cannot understand that you
An Oogly - Woogly bird don't know
The tail is made of coloured strips
Please will you make them curl?
And perhaps stick them on just there?
It's a bit hard for a little girl

The wings are made of the feathers
That we collected on our walk
But please mummy don't expect
The Oogly - Woogly bird to talk'
When it was finished, it was grand
It surpassed the peacock bird
*'I didn't know that. Oh, how absurd'*
The mother's voice was softly heard

# Once In A While

Could I have what I want?
Just once in a while
That would be so different
You would see me smile

Why does no one listen?
Just once in a while
I want to do such a lot
For you I'd run a mile

Will someone ask me?
Just once in a while
Is my name invisible?
Or not on any file?

Should I just stop hoping?
It's been such a while
Get my needs and wishes
And make a rubbish pile?

All my thoughts and ideas
Make my life go by

**BUT**

Just once in a while
**You may see me cry**

# Normal Reaction

I am a sad person
To be happy I try
People ignore me
I don't know why
I will help anyone
I am quite kind
I give my time
And I do not mind
What makes me sad
Well-
I fell down one day
Those who saw me
Just turned away
They didn't give back
Any bit that I gave
Instead walked past
Not even a wave

I am a sad person
Do you understand?
As no one noticed
I needed a hand
I used to be happy
Before I was ill
I was liked then
As needs I could fill
But-
Once I was empty
My task was done
No one gave thought
I needed some fun
Support and comfort
Time and a place
At any table I need
Just a very small space

# Sunshine

S is for the Sun, it is shining  bright

U is for an Umbrella, now rolled up so tight

N is for the Nuisance of the rain today

S is for a Sandwich we had to put away

H is for our Hurry, to stay quite warm and dry

I is for the Instructions, to obey -we had to try

N is for the Naughty cloud, it just came our way

E is for the Enjoyment, we all had today


Our picnic can now really start, and we can have some fun
The cloud has been blown away, no damage has been done
We shall not eat soggy bread, our biscuits are still crisp
The lemonade is not spilt, and little time is missed

We did not let that black cloud spoil the special day for us
We all just ate our tea and did not make a fuss
The ground dried up in no time as the sun began to shine
We soon forgot the rain and had a lovely time

What a difference sunshine makes with its brilliant light
It changes a very gloomy day into one so bright
A rainbow is the sky's wide smile when rain stops pouring down
Something we all like to see –

**-better than a big dark frown**

# My Bike

I loved my bike, it was the best
That I had ever seen
It was not a new one
I never knew whose it had been
Adult wheels, just three gears
The chrome polished till it shone
Black framework, nothing fancy
Though a bell was fitted on
It had been repainted
But I just didn't care
For to me – it was 'freedom'
To me – 'wind in my hair'
Dirt tracking on the common
Picnics to the park
But I had no bike lights
So was always home by dark
I had a tin, a puncture kit
I carried everywhere
I didn't know how to use it
But felt safe that it was there
The basket on the front
Held groceries from the shop
We lived in hilly country
You've guessed - right at the top
When the wind was blowing
I would be too puffed to talk
Trying really hard to peddle
I would sometimes have to walk
Little traffic on the roads
Made biking such a pleasure
For my happiest hours of childhood
I remember that bike - for ever

# Trying Hard

The staircase is very high
At the top I see a door
The steps just go on and on
I must climb some more

No handrail to assist me
It is quite out of reach
I climb up the best I can
That is what they teach

When I get to the top
I have just had a thought
If I find the door is closed
All this will be for nought

All my effort, all my fear
I try hard, I really try
But if I can't get through
That's when I shall cry

I don't think little legs
Should have to climb at all
I want to be carried
Until I grow quite tall

That is not the way of life
**Success** you have to earn
**Trying hard** is a lesson
**Reward** is what you learn

# The Carousel

What do you see from the Carousel?
As you go round and round
Mums and Dads all waiting
For their children on the ground

What do you see from the Carousel?
On the pony painted white
Over hills and valleys
You get such a  lovely sight

What do you see from the Carousel?
Do you see fields of green?
Or do you see the steps on board
Where many feet have been?

What do you see from the Carousel?
As you  hear the music play
When night has come all around
The lights still seem like day

What do you see from the Carousel?
I remember at the fair
A special time of laughter
That day was ours to share

What you saw from the Carousel
Memories - of laughter, joy and fun
These can blow black clouds away
And help bring back your sun

# My Hobby

The needles clatter quickly
I am knitting very fast
The jumper will be lovely
I hope that it will last
It is an achievement
Something that I can see
For all the hours I put in
I've made it just for me

I have knitted for my sister
My baby brother too
For myself I have found
Time, and this wool so blue
It is just the perfect colour
I shall wear it with great pride
Outdoors in the snow and wind
If too thick to wear inside

I was taught to knit and sew
When young, I am so glad
As I have had so many days
When alone and very sad
If I am sitting by myself
And can not go out all day
I just pick up my needles
And knit the hours away

# My Horse

'I shall ride a big brown horse'
'But your legs are still so small'
'Yes but they are very strong
And one day I'll be quite tall'

'I shall have a big brown horse'
'Where do you want to ride?'
'Just anywhere and everywhere'
The small girl said with pride

'I shall care for my big brown horse'
'You must do that every day'
'I shall brush him well at night
And feed him bags of hay'

'If you have a big brown horse
I hope you take great care'
'I shall guide him carefully
To fall off I would not dare'

'Why do you want a big brown horse
In the future -for you to ride?'
'I do not know - but I just do
And that wish I cannot hide'

'I dreamed I had a big brown horse
I rode him quickly up a hill
I woke and he had disappeared
Maybe I long to find him still'

# The Little Train

**1.**
Round and round went the train
Past the station, on and on
'Where are we going all day long?'
'On and on till the journey's done'

**2.**
'Round and round, nothing changes
What is this, some kind of game?'
'Only when I make it change
Will the journey not be the same'

**3.**
'Round and round every day
But the track, it never alters'
The wheels still go on and on
If the little train never falters

**4.**
'This is nonsense, on and on
Round and round, the same'
'Well, it needs but little effort
And I like my journey game'

**5.**
The train has stopped, deary me
Something broke the track
'Help is here' the driver said
'We shall soon be speeding back'

**6.**
'Back to where, what and when?
Where we go is round and round'
'Yes, but going round and round
We can cover lots of ground'

**7.**
'A different way I want to go
Do I need a different track?'
'No only a few small changes
But there will be no going back'

**8.**
'I shall change the track today
More ideas then I must find
To make my new journey
But I have plenty in my mind'

**9.**
'Round and round, on and on
The same, no effort needed
But it was getting very dull
So your comments I have heeded'

**10.**
'It's exciting, and do you know
My train now joins in races
Over mountains and open plains
Across bridges – to other places'

# Lost Opportunity

**I'm not joking when I tell you this**

I wrote a simply brilliant poem
Judged, of course by me
But my computer ate it
Now it's nowhere I can see
All the words were written
With my eyes quite full of tears
Gone, somewhere, I don't know
Moving lines - about my fears

Like the fish that 'got away'
It really was the best
The words were very powerful
It surpassed all of the rest
But I cannot recall the verses
That vanished with such speed
Would a few computing lessons
Let me learn just what I need?

What a waste, I am so sorry
A masterpiece down the drain
The only thing that I remember
Its going gave a 'sudden pain'
All that outpouring - gone for good
I must really take more care
Or who will ever read my poems?
Or my raw emotions share?

# Mummy's Message

I do the best that I can do
I love you all the same
But I am one and you are (three)
I cannot play in every game

My hands are often very full
They cannot hold another
That doesn't mean I love you less
Than your sister or your brother

I give you all my time to use
Each day for you I care
But you will all have to learn
My hands you have to share

There is no cloud that hides you
In my heart a sun shines bright
It lights up all your pathways
It glows both day and night

Just have a little patience
I see you and love you all
If you don't all shout at once
I can hear your every call

Let's have fun together
Share our time and understand
I love you, each one the same

**BUT**

**I don't have another hand**

# The Rocking Horse

**1.**
I wish I had a rocking horse
Of shining wood, well made
With a saddle of brown leather
And a mane that will not fade

**2.**
I would maybe call him Beauty
Or Dobbin or Silver Moon
Jack or Moses or Shining Star
I would find the right name soon

**3.**
People really need to know
A rocking horse can't decide
How fast to go on its runners
When it takes you for a ride

**4.**
It all depends how big it is
And who sits upon its back
Whether you hold the reins tight
Or relax and leave them slack

**5.**
I would travel over many hills
Sometimes ride above tall trees
I'd try to race the birds that fly
But avoid the swarms of bees

**6.**
My imagination would take me
Anywhere I longed to be
Spend rainy days in warm lands
But be always home for tea

**7.**
My horse would quietly whisper
If I urged him to go too far
'My legs are very tired, you know
You really should go by car'

**8.**
When we spend time together
He would stop me being lonely
Pretending to gallop over fields
As if he **was** a real live pony

**9.**
But I don't have a rocking horse
No one my voice will heed
So instead I'll do a jigsaw
And hide away my need

**10.**
My horse will have to wait until
Some day when I am married
Then I shall buy a special one
To give to the one I carried

# Mrs Squirrel

Dear Mrs Squirrel

You can not use my loft
I know it's safe and warm
And the lagging is so soft
But, no, you can't persuade me
No matter how you try
This is my home not yours
There are many reasons why

You have no personal hygiene
The wet patch on my ceiling
Showed you have no respect
It was really quite revealing
If you had the same standards
I could possibly let you share
But you have such dirty habits
And you obviously do not care

But also, you never asked
You thought you had the right
To invade my personal space
And came in the dark of night
You brought only hassle
Finding you made me upset
You caused a lot of damage
The worst vermin I have met

There are many empty barns
Old sheds and hollow trees
Build your nest somewhere else
Where in winter you won't freeze
I have netted all the openings
Replaced wood you found to chew
Finally, understand this message
I will never live with you

# My Animals

A monkey rides on the rhino's back
Wolves chat patiently in the sun
The lion sits with the sheep
While lambs gambol, having fun
Together sharing dinner
The cat and dog eat in peace
The elephant's long trunk splashes
The hippo's dry back to ease
The peacock's tail gives shelter
For two rabbits in the rain
The cheetah sleeps, while a porcupine
Grooms the white wild horse's mane
The giraffe reaches for high fruit
The gorilla would like to eat
And in the dusk they sing a song
At the waterhole as they meet

When I play with my animals
Each has a simple task
Wooden, they can not argue
And do just what I ask

# Things That Cannot Be Bought

I saw a man, he had a coat, like gold it shone so clear
I asked him where he bought it, and had it cost him dear?
'You cannot buy a coat like this', he replied to me
'It is called **Courage**, but it did not come free
I went through a field of pain, I got to the other side
I had no one to help me and no horse for me to ride'

I saw a man with a hat, it looked like a silver moon
I asked him where he bought it, and could I get one soon?
'You cannot buy a hat like this', he replied to me
It is called **Kindness,** and it did not come free
I helped one who was lost, and one who could not walk
One who had no food or drink, and one too ill to talk

I saw a man with shiny boots, strong, light - as if a feather
I asked him where he bought them, he said he hadn't -ever
'You cannot buy boots like these', he replied to me
They are called **Endurance**, and they did not come free
I had to work beyond my strength, and for so very long
No other there to lift the load, and no help came along

I saw a man with a light, that shone out far and bright
I asked him where he bought it, as it beamed into the night
You cannot buy a light like this, he replied to me
It is called eternal **Hope,** it was given to me- free
I had lost direction, I had battled to the end
I had coped when all was lost, for myself I had to fend

Then a light I suddenly saw, upon my darkest day
I did not ask, it was just there, and then I found my way
You have to find your **Courage**
        **Kindness** comes from very deep
        **Endurance** needs much effort

      but

      **Hope** is yours - to keep

# Imagination

The pictures I get in my mind
Sometimes are not very kind
They make me fear
I shed a tear        - **but**
They are different to what I find

The dog seemed very big and tall
When it jumped upon the wall
I ran in fright
Oh, what a sight   - **but**
It didn't come near to me at all

To see the dentist I didn't dare
Those pictures gave me a scare
I had a pain
Then bad again      - **but**
He didn't hurt - I wasn't fair

In my stomach a knot seems tied
Now - that can not be denied
*'If you let it ease*
*The fear will cease'* - **oh**
That is something I haven't tried

I think it is if I don't know
Then my brain the worst will show
I usually cry
Though I don't try   - **well**
*'Use courage- then just 'have a go'*

If I listen to what is said
Before making pictures in my head
I'll make anew
A better view        - **then – yes**
I could be quite calm instead

**I think so**

# Baking Day

No one baked like she did
Her pastry was just divine
Scones melted in the mouth
Macaroons were pretty fine
Demarara buns aplenty
Congress tarts to fill a tin
Chocolate cake 'to die for'
I ate them all -and I was thin

In the pantry I'd have a peak
Take a big deep breath to savour
The delights we would have to eat
Oh, our Mum did us a favour
Thursday was her 'baking day'
No tart allowed to burn
Started when to school we went
Completed by our return

Every week it was the same
She stayed at home with pride
To feed her flock was her task
No one better, far or wide
But I had the biggest shock
When I grew up and went away
Hard pastry and tasteless cakes
I didn't know it was that way

Little we had in childhood years
Such havoc war had wrought
But no one could take away
The talent our Mother brought
At home to greet us every day
Her food passed any test
Material things we may not have
But we ate 'the very best'

Nowadays, eating all the cakes
The scones, mince pies or bun
Would not be a good idea
As getting fat is not much fun
But then we used the energy
Without mobile phone or car
No one could fetch or carry
We just walked or cycled far

# Little Things

Freshly made loaves of bread, baked in tiny tins for tea
Will someone who reads this poem know who did that for me?

Learning how to weed the garden, what to pull and what to save
Will someone who reads this poem know the one whose time she gave?

Ladybirds walking on stalks of grass, bring back memories of you
Will someone who reads this poem know who I'm talking to?

Walking in the fields of grass, collecting mushrooms in the dew
Will someone who reads this poem know if we gathered 'just a few'?

Listening to the birds sing, in the hedgerows as we walk
Will someone who reads this poem know the one of whom I talk?

Never too busy at any time to listen as a young child chattered
Will someone who reads this poem know the one to whom it mattered?

Not the most important things to happen in this world
But to that child it simply meant being seen and being heard

# Playing A Game

Do you play a game to win?
Or do you play to play?
Does losing upset you?
There is still another day
You can always be alone
No one to share your game
But then, alas, tomorrow
It will just be the same

It is fun to play a game
Win or lose or draw
If playing is all the fun
You will play some more
But if losing upsets you
And makes you walk away
Then the fun will disappear
And no game another day

# Santa

I cannot wait till morning
Do you think he'll find the way?
Will he know there is another
This year - for toys to play?
I have written him a letter
Asking for a doll for me
And a teddy for my brother
In the cot, I hope he'll see

I wouldn't like him to be missed
Because he can't yet talk
I have explained to Santa
That he is too young to walk
So, if he puts both by the tree
To open his first, I'll try
And then he can play with it
And he won't need to cry

Santa, please make the paper
Be not too strong or tight
I have only little fingers
And I ought to rest tonight
Instead of thinking to disturb
Mum and dad if they're asleep
As when you've been I think
I may just need to have a peep

Santa's been and I now write
A little thank you letter
My brother loves his teddy
And my doll could not be better
I cuddled his teddy for a while
To make sure it was alright
Then I went back to bed and
Opened mine when it came light

# A Bird

In times gone by, life was tough
For children who were ill
No medicines to make them well
Just days in bed, keeping still

§

'Who are you?' the child was asked
She thought - so hard she tried
'I know the name I'm given'
She said - and then she cried
'I am a pet lamb to my Daddy
I am 'naughty' to my Mum
I am a nuisance to my brother
And I rarely have much fun
A bossy sister to another
A nursemaid to the third
But most of all I am ill
And I wish I was a bird

I would fly over every tree
To see what lies beyond
This quiet little village which
Doesn't **even** have a pond
I think my world is really
A very small place to be
It could be better, I am sure, if
Something different I could see
But, really, I do nothing
My life is quite absurd
I just cough and wheeze daily

Yes -
        - I wish I was a bird'

# Daydreams

I like to think I am strong
I like to think I am brave
I like to think I could be
A person who could save
Someone from a burning house
Someone in a boat about to sink
Someone who was desperate
I just like to think

I would like to be quite strong
I would like to be quite brave
I would like to be someone
Who could another save
How can I be different?
When I am stuck in bed
I can be anything, anywhere
But only in my head

Someone said that I am strong
Someone said that I am brave
Someone said that I am kind
And I don't need to save
All I need is to carry on
With the courage I have so deep
That was really good to hear, so
Now those words I'll keep

# Friends

The teddy bear sat on the little boy's bed
He looked sad as sad can be
'Why can't I join in someone's game?
Why will no one play with me?'

The doll sat on the little girl's bed
She looked sad as sad can be
'I want to join in that game now
But no one ever shows me how'

*The toys said:-*

'Why do they quarrel?
Why do they fight?'
'We watch and see
It doesn't feel right'

'I wish we could leave
Our beds and walk
I would say what I think
If I could talk'

'They could be like us
Friends who can share
I wonder if they hear us?
It's really not fair'

The little girl and boy came back
They were having a picnic tea
The doll and bear went in their pack
They were happy as could be

*The toys said:-*

'Did they hear us?
I cannot wait
A picnic tea ?
That is just great'

'They are now friends'
'Yes, their smiles show
'They are having fun'
'That's good to know'

# A Pain

If I get a tummy ache, or a pain I do not like
The sort of pain that stops me from riding on my bike
Then I roll up, get into bed, and for a while I'll stay
And pretend that I can make the pain go right away

I become a bright red ball and bounce right off the bed
Down the stairs, through the door, go play with friends instead
I can bounce wherever - in sun, rain, wind or snow
To the park to feed the ducks, help Dad his lawn to mow

To the seaside far away, to dig castles in the sand
In stormy sea I sail a boat, on a treasure island land
Sometimes I choose a circus, I swing on the trapeze
The crowds all cheer as I fly by, over their heads with ease

I can ride across the moors, on a pony fast and sure
It jumps the streams and heather, its coat is white and pure
I climb the highest mountain, alone and very brave
See someone who is stranded and help their life to save

I visit other countries, in tall trees with monkeys play
Anything I don't like, well then, I just bounce away
I do it when I need to, I just shut my eyes, decide
What I want to be and do, and away go on a ride

There is nothing I cannot do, I've been just everywhere
My favourites I return to and they are always there
My imagination helps me to forget about the pain
And only when it's gone away

                    do I bounce back again

# Bullied

'Why are you frightened little one?
And why do your tears now fall?'
'I was hit by some children
Much bigger and so tall'

'Why would that ever happen
To a kind sweet child like you?
'I don't know, they didn't say
Except horrid things they'd do'

'What did you do, little one?
Did you try to run away?'
'I was not able to move my legs
And so I had to stay'

'Did you fight and hit back?
You may be small but strong'
'I did not want to hurt them
And they might have carried on'

'One day they will learn a lesson
It need not come from you
Someday they will feel exactly
The same as you went through

In the meantime, I now know
And I will watch out for you
Their actions will be punished
Nothing more allowed to do

Let fear and anger disappear
One day they will need aid
Some pain will then remind them
That a big mistake they made

**All bullies will need others help
All bullies can suffer pain
All bullies need food and drink
All things come round again'**

# Alarm Clock

I have to get up early, my alarm clock carefully set
I sleep so very peacefully, when such a fright I get
If it rings suddenly, its noise makes me really jump
I sometimes fall out of bed and get a nasty bump

But if I don't have it there or forget to set it right
I might be late for school – or not ready, nice and bright
I may miss the school bus, my friends will go without
Play where I don't know, and never hear me shout

I would rather sleep all night and dream the hours away
If I thought I'd oversleep, then awake I know I'd stay
So, I've just bought a clock that plays music soft and sweet
I open my eyes more slowly, now get out on my feet

It's a calmer way to meet the day, better than a rush
Otherwise the morning seems just all pull and push
Getting shouted at to wash, to eat my breakfast up
To dress myself quickly, drink 'properly' from my cup

Not to mess my blouse up, spill cornflakes on my skirt
Not to waste the toothpaste, or splash my brother's shirt
It's far better to be wide awake before I wander down
And if I am quite early, I miss both scowl and frown

A smile to start the day makes the sun appear to shine
I can do my school work, and play with friends just fine
People seem more kind when I 'think' before I 'do'
That makes such a difference-

**-is it the same for you?**

65

# The Pear Tree

The pear tree stood triumphant
Tall, wide and full of bloom
Like a ship with big white sails
But was it sailing to its doom?

**Well, nearly as:-**

### 1.

A west wind did blow so hard
And caused the tree to sway
It looked as though it would fall
And their home was in its way
'Oh dear. What shall we do?
What about the fruit it bears?'
*'If we don't cut the branches down*
*Our house will need repairs'*

### 2.

'Yes, that is more important'
They all easily agreed, so
Daringly, the tree was pruned
Even while the wind did blow
The main tree still remained
So the swings were not affected
But the mess on the floor looked
As if scaffolding was erected

### 3.

The branches laying on the ground
Were climbed by girls and boys
Who forgot about their dolls
And cars and **all** their other toys
They gave many hours of pleasure
And were safer 'off the tree'
The children had fun all summer
And played – happy as could be

### 4.

They did not mind not having
Fresh pears to eat for tea
No, these games were better
It became their favourite tree
The tree survived, its old roots
Settled in the earth with ease
Blossom came in future years
With pears - to cook and freeze

**But, do you know?**

Never again did that tree
Give such a lot of pleasure
As the year the strong westerlies
Nearly blew it down for ever

# Patience and Courage

'Where did you find **Patience**?'
The little girl asked her mother
'I think it was when ill in bed
And couldn't meet with any other
I tried to wait, tried not to mind
Long days passed slowly by
Then a part of me was there
Said I could -if I should try
So she helped me make pictures
Of things that I would do
We talked about having good times
She helped me to get through'

'Where did you find **Courage**?'
The father was asked by his son
'It was never ever easy, and
I once thought that he had gone
Then one night some bombs fell
I had a dreadful scare
It made him wake up suddenly
And I knew that he was there
I ran through the dark street
To reach help for us that night
And he guided me onwards
Though there was no light'

'How shall we find patience?
Do we have to be ill in bed?'
'No, you have our example
Learn from us', the mother said
'You cannot always do as you like
Listen, hear and never mind
The only time you should be cross
Is if people are not kind
Then you need Father's courage
To stick up for what is right
Patience and courage are part of you

But I hope -

            - **you** will never need to fight'

# At The End Of The Day

When I go to bed I ponder. What have I done this day I wonder?
How did I behave each hour? As a selfish weed or lovely flower?
Have I been busy with some task? Was it quite useful work? I ask
Did I use the day quite well? Have I anything myself to tell?

Was I serious or did I smile? For someone walk the extra mile?
Did I fall, kept head up high? Was I relaxed or heaved a sigh?
We all have a finite limit - I do not want to waste a minute
Life can be hard for me or you - we all have lots of things to do

It is so lovely to be happy. I hate it if I am quite snappy
But life is not a bunch of roses, sometimes people 'get up noses'
Maybe when you look you'll find, that to someone you were kind
Or maybe you had a pain, and just went back to bed again

When I go to sleep at night, I have not always got it right
But I have learned to use my days - in so many varied ways
Do the same, look and see – and maybe different you could be
Bad times pass, they go away. Learn, so **you** don't make them stay

Some days we may smile or cry - others we don't want to try
We can all make mistakes - the main thing is we are not fakes
Be not too critical or severe, just listen to yourself and hear
What has been, how it's been done and -

was any battle lost or won?

**You decide**

**Will tomorrow be different?**

# Nature

What kind of flower would I be
If I had not come here as me?
What lovely colour would I choose?
There are so many, I couldn't lose

Would I have a fragrant smell?
Or like a rose have thorns as well?
Would I be dainty, pretty and small?
The lily of the valley has them all
An autumn flower, colourful, strong?
A bold chrysanthemum blooming long?
A sunflower reaching to the light
Standing proud, its colour bright?
A Dahlia boasting many blooms
Holding the stage in many rooms?
Beautiful, stylish, an orchid be
Exquisite, just a joy to see?
A freesia delicate, fragrant, sweet
As lovely as ever you could meet?
There are hundreds I could mention
I give just a few for your attention!

I would not want to be a weed
They do not ever seem to heed
The needs of other plants around
And just take over any ground
As if a random hand has thrown
When pulled up, again have grown
And everywhere they do appear
Carelessly spreading with no fear
Without a care, giving no joy
Not even beauty do they employ
Arrogant, selfish all the way
Not giving, just taking every day

Flowers and weeds are all around
On this earth, growing in the ground
If you could chose
What would **you** be?

**What would we all get to see?**

# Soon

Please can you tell me?
How long must I wait for 'soon?'
Will it be today?
Before I see the rising moon?
Or tomorrow or the next day
Or maybe -in a week?
When will you let me know
The answer that I seek?

I am tired of hoping
I am weary to my toes
From the ends of all my fingers
My energy now flows
Please make 'soon' be near to now
Not in a long, long time
Will it be in the morning?
Before the sun can shine?

If I give you three pennies
Will that bring 'soon' to here?
I cannot keep asking
It could stretch another year
Is your time like mine
Sometimes quick but often slow
I have now a worry

**If 'soon' comes – how shall I know?**

# Temper Tantrums

There is something very strange that I want to share with you
Sometimes a little monster comes, a lot of damage it can do

The other day I was playing with friends and it really wasn't fair
One minute I was in the game, the next, a monster there

It ranted and it raved so much, it tore my book, it threw my train
It shouted and it screamed and, then, it did it all again

It wasn't like a goblin, it wasn't strange like that
It didn't have great big feet or wear a funny hat

I couldn't believe it at first, whatever could this be
The strangest thing of all was, it looked like another me

From my socks right to my shirt, it wore clothes just like me
How did mine get so crumpled, I got dressed as tidy as can be

It stayed there quite a long time, and then it went away
How do I know it will not come back and spoil another day

I do not know where it came from, I don't want it to appear
But I don't know where it lives, whether far away or near

I don't want my friends to leave, I don't want my books all torn
I don't want to play alone. Oh dear -
                                        I'm left - feeling all forlorn

A monster? That looks like me? I ask, how can that be?
I am a nice child, very sweet

**Please**

**Please, don't think it's me**

# The Necklace

I have a coloured necklace, the first stone is of blue
It reminds me of **Courage**, bad times to battle through
I needed it when I was small, and when I couldn't walk
If I was ill and couldn't breathe - enough to even talk

The next stone is of yellow – it reminds me of a laugh
**Humour**, is a bright light that shines on any path
Sometimes we need to see life in a different way
Or disappointment comes and often wants to stay

Emerald green follows – the colour of fields of grass
When I think of outdoors, **Imagination's** pictures pass
I needed this ability when confined to bed for ages
I created lots of scenes to fill my empty pages

Pink is my **Patient** stone – its colour seems at peace
When I look at it my mind soon starts to feel at ease
I needed it when exhausted with trying hard to live
I would sit and quietly wait – a stone no one can give

**Hope** is purple, a beautiful shade – it stands out from the rest
It gives life its meaning, it really is the best
I have needed it every day that was difficult to survive
Made me see a future and remember I was alive

The necklace I wear with great pride, a record of my life
If anything is difficult, I hold the stone that fits the strife
Then I believe - I can do my best - for yet another day
As I have done it all before, and managed it - my way

# The Squirrels

The squirrel woke each morning
And thought – 'Oh what a lovely day'
He went to call on all his friends
And they went out to play
They chased each other on the fence
And raced from tree to tree
They ran all over the flower beds
As happy as could be

When they were feeling hungry
They sat and munched a nut
They usually hid a few each day
But forgot where they were put
They jumped at the dog and cat
And away the birds all flew
They raced about in the afternoon
As lots of games they knew

Some of the nuts which they buried
Were never ever found
And little trees soon appeared
Long roots deep in the ground
Amongst flowers, beans and lettuces
In the potato patch they grew
To remove them the gardener
Had a lot of work to do

Nothing harmed the squirrels
They were never short of food
They always had each other
And for them - all days were good
But for the cat
        and the dog
        and the birds
        and gardener too

The squirrels were just little pests

**What would they be for you?**

# What Am I Worth

What am I worth?
The little child said
Am I only as good
As the hair on my head?
The nose on my face?
My smile and my tears?
Am I worth more?
Those are my fears

What am I worth?
The little child said
Do you know what
I think in my head?
Can you see courage?
As I battle through
Can you see any good
In all that I do?

What am I worth?
The little child said
You cannot judge
By what I've read
You need to know
The 'me' inside
Then you can own
Your child with pride

# The Acer

I was given a bronze leaved tree
Acer is its family's name
Most plants like the sunshine
I thought this would do the same

I planted it in the garden
In full view, for all to see
But it didn't like the new place
And quite soon it 'spoke' to me

It could not talk, as no tree can
Our language it doesn't know
But it just had to tell me
It used another way to show

It dropped its leaves one by one
As it faced the morning sun
As though to say, 'I prefer the shade'
So an understanding was begun

In a quiet corner, now protected
It gets light but also shade
It grew next year and do you know?
Such a beautiful sight it made

The dull corner was transformed
By its prettiness all day long
With our care it is growing well
And I'm sure will be quite strong

A bolder tree is now planted
In the place I chose before
It seems to like that situation
And will have flowers in galore

Some people flourish in limelight
Some prefer to live in shade
All are important in life's garden
Where all varieties are made

# Wishes

A child stood at the wishing well
Eyes closed tight as tight can be
She threw her coin and down it fell
'Please hear this wish from me'

'I want to stay a little longer
Please, will you make it true?
Can I play a few more games?
This is all I ask of you

Make us not go home yet
We shall leave them all behind
And I shall miss them very much
They really are so kind'

She dried her tears and smiled
Then she heard a clear voice say
'Flight 201 has been cancelled'
'Hurrah, we shall have to stay'

So, the little girl got her wish
Foggy weather was to blame
But to her it seemed like magic
And the result was just the same

# Boredom

What is boredom? What does it mean?
How can it come about?
Would someone who knows please tell me?
And I'll try to sort it out

I look around and I just marvel
At the things that I can see
Every flower is different and
So is every single tree

No person is just like the next
And even twins can vary
So how can boredom play a part?
I find that rather scary

Interest is in all around
Even things that bring me strife
I think if I was ever bored
I would be missing out on life

Little things could be overlooked
That bring their joy to me
A smile amid the stress and gloom
A light that some don't see

Life is made up of small moments
Added together to make the whole
So if you don't want to be bored
Gather them all –
                          **or take the toll**

# Seals

Why do I love watching seals?
I really can not tell
Is it because in water
They can swim and dive so well?
They have such trusting faces
With their lovely big brown eyes
They look just like a family pet
Who has had a big surprise

With a sudden movement
They depart, so sleek and fast
They travel under water far
What a long time they can last
Yet on the land they are clumsy
With flippers short and small
The big tail seems so heavy
When they climb on rocks so tall

Basking in the sunshine
Within their world, no care
Maybe we just envy that
And would like a bit to share
I don't know, it's a puzzle
But whenever near the sea
I find the likely places
That seals may wish to be

Then I sit and watch them
And sometimes, as I walk
I look in their eyes directly
And pretend to me they talk
They tell me all about the sea
And the fish they catch to eat
I wonder if they understand
I'm so pleased when we can meet

# Plans

I have plans for every morning
Something special for each day
But when I wake, they always
Turn around and run away

In my head I work so hard
Do everything very fast
But when I wake, someone else
For all the fun is cast

It isn't that I change my mind
No - I am not to blame
As other people interfere
It really is a shame

They may say 'wait till tomorrow'
Or 'only when you grow old'
So, in my days are <u>their</u> plans
As I do what I am told

I shall put mine away safely
Into a big box - to wait
But I wonder, when I get old
Will it all then be to late?

# The Yellow Teaset

### 1.

It was of brightest yellow
So wonderful to see
A teapot, cups and saucers
To give some dollies tea
This could be a sad tale
I'll leave you to decide
'I have no dolls to play with'
Her tears she tried to hide
The box that held the teaset
Had an accident and fell
You can guess what happened
I do not have to tell

### 2.

Some children are given much
Many toys that they can choose
This young girl had very little
Now, nothing left to lose
She pretended she had dollies
To play with on the floor
She made up lots of games
And then imagined more
But there was a silver lining
She was never, ever bored
Because she must amuse herself
Her brain was not ignored

### 3.

No time spent disappointed
Or lost on wasted wishes
She had to do many things
To dust, wash dirty dishes
Childhood is for learning
For playing and for fun
Sometimes that is impossible
Was there any damage done?
When there is little to be had
Then work is joined to play
This was a war-time child
Who struggled through each day

### 4.

Nothing was taken for granted
Nothing expected, little gained
But a richness grew unnoticed
Inner talents were obtained
Time was spent discovering
And practising many a skill
Knitting, sewing, an old bike
Endless daylight hours to fill
No television, no CDs made
By pop-idols by the score
No MP3s, or videos

**But - do you know?**

**In those days**

**No child thought to ask for 'more'**

# Harmony

### 1.
Did you see the snow?
Shining very white
That is how it fell down
From the sky at night
It is like a facecloth
Fluffy and so clean
Covering all the tracks
Where little feet have been

### 2.
Can the squirrel find
Its food hidden deep?
Can the robin hop away
And its watch still keep?
Does the prowling cat
Sink into the snow?
Can the rabbit find its hole?
I really do not know

### 3.
It happens every winter
But each year it is the same
Rabbits eat our lettuces
They think it is a game
Nut trees grow everywhere
Cats come and make a mess
So I think the answers
Must be 'yes, yes and yes

### 4.
'What about the Robin?'
'Oh, I heard him while at play'

*He said:-*

'The snow looked very pretty
And it only stayed a day
In the branches of the tree
I sat and then I fed
Thank you for all the crumbs
From your cake and bread'

### 5.
The garden must be a safe place
Where he can hop each day

*So I said:-*

'I will send the cat back home
And the squirrel shoo away
If you have any problems
With rabbits -let me know
Then we can live together and
Watch the garden grow'

# The Wind

I can hear the wind blowing
Making a lot of noise
It takes the leaves off the trees
They fall and have no choice.
It blows the sea into big waves
The clouds move very fast
To walk becomes quite difficult
How long is it going to last?

I cannot see the wind at all
Where does it start and go?
It blows and is so very strong
What makes it? I don't know
Has it come a long way?
And will it now go far?
Maybe it came in the night
And travelled on a star

There are people far away
Very dear, I cannot see
I am going to ask this wind
To carry love from me
I shall put kisses in its path
They can travel in the air
If they ever reach them
Then a moment we shall share

So blow wind, but gently
In your arms my kisses bear
If one gets lost on the way
I have plenty left to spare
Blow softly on her little cheek
Onto his short cropped hair
When you do, let them know
That I wish that I was there

# Boys And Girls

I was born and I was told
I came all in a rush
I heard that storks carried boys
To under a gooseberry bush

They had not to wash dishes
Or put away their toys
No, those were jobs for little girls
Not for little boys

Boys could say what they want
Be naughty and even rage
But little girls must obey
Behave well at any age

You may think this unfair
Or even rather bad
But I learned many things
And now I am quite glad

If chores made me angry
Gooseberry prickles came to mind
Poor things, I would think
And then I could be kind

I just looked and I listened
Till now - said not one word
But I never found that bush
Stork's wings I never heard

So I didn't believe it at all
The difference was quite clear
Girls learn to do many things
And boys seldom shed a tear

# Grandma's Apples

My grandma had an orchard
With many apple trees
Rabbits came to play there
As did lots of buzzing bees
But also would come children
From the village houses near
One incident upset me greatly
Caused me to shed a tear

Someone said we should eat
Grandma's apples without asking
They were green and very sour
Munched, while sitting, basking
Punishment came along
'Stomach ache' was it's name
It let me know it had not been
The best or wisest game

In my deepest heart I knew
In this game we were not honest
Taking apples that were not mine
Seemed to break a trust or promise
But from that awful feeling
I learned a strong belief

**Never let others make you do
Anything to cause you grief**

# The Copper Beech Tree

Growing tall and wide and brown
Is a magnificent copper beech
Planted by an English queen
Its branches now are out of reach
The legend is that Victoria
Had this task-one day in May
She must have done it very well
As it stands beautiful- to this day

It grew and grew, quite slowly
For a hundred years - now old
I guess that if it could speak
A lot of stories could be told
I wonder how many people
Have passed beneath its shade?
Did some eat a picnic there
Or took photos that now fade?

Did the postman bring letters
Past its trunk in days gone by?
Did people meet to laugh and talk
Sheltering from a sunny sky?
The people who lived all around
Have changed or moved away
On nearby land are new houses
But-
that same tree is here to stay

**Will it be here for another hundred years**

**What do you think?**

# School Trip To The Seaside

We went on the coach early
To the seaside for the day
The sandwiches packed for lunch
Were all eaten on the way
The money given for icecream
Was wasted with no gain
As we visited the slot machines
While hiding from the rain

Two got lost in the crowd
So we held each others' hands
While the teachers did a search
So we never saw the sands
We set off back at 5 o'clock
Hungry, cold and wet
*'Did you have a good day'?*

**'No – one I wish I could forget'**

I had hoped to paddle
In the sea, so rarely seen
Dig in the sand, sit in the sun
Remember where I'd been
But I can't tell you the place, or
Who took me there that day
I think I was just too young
What a pity it was that way

Not knowing where I was
I remember being afraid
So, instead of fun and happiness
A worrying path was made
Some experiences could easily wait
Till understanding comes with age
As once written in our memory
We may keep an unforgettable page

# Favourite Place

As far as the eye can see
Sand, shingle and more sand
Distant hills across water deep
Endless sky above my hand

Gannets with graceful flight
Waiting moments, then so swift
Oyster catchers, gulls and terns
Appear, dancing in the drift

In patchy fog ships become
Ghostly vessels in the sky
In sunshine, the vistas change
Treasures money could not buy

All I can say is, that somehow
Even when the mist can hide
In my opinion, this favourite place
Is the best nature can provide

Others must not feel its magic
Isolation comes to my mind
As whenever I can walk there
Few other people do I find

When preferred is other noise
Not the calls of birds and sea
Loud music, many companions
Then this beauty is left for me

I will not say what is its name
Or where this place you'd find
Its solitude may be removed
A treasure stolen from my mind

# Going To Sleep

I am tired, really tired
The day has been quite long
I feel my eyes shutting
In my ears I hear a song
I am singing to myself
No one else can hear
When I sing within my head
Sleep will soon come near

I like going to my bed
Whatever the day was like
I may have played with my friends
Or been riding on my bike
But when I am very tired
The best thing I can do
Is say 'goodnight', start a song
And sleep the whole night through

I think 'sleep' likes my songs
I have a favourite few
Sometimes I manage one
But occasionally get to two
Into dreamland I arrive
Have a few adventures there
Get back in time for morning
And for another day prepare

# Goblins

'I don't like being in darkness
Even a star I cannot see
Or a light that glimmers
So alone, no one with me

Goblins appear in my mind
They are here, they are so near'
'Those are not real, understand
They are created by your fear'

'I cry and no one comforts me
I think I must be bad'
'Feel my arm around you
You are feeling very sad'

'I could shout, I could scream
And hit them just the same'
'Try to put it into words
As anger is its name

You have faced those goblins
And made them go away
Rest quietly and sleep the night
Till you meet another day

You are only very young
You'll grow up when you can
And you will learn how to be
A kind and gentle man'

# Cleaning The Attic

I will clean the attic, not done since I was small
Full of memorabilia, how did I get it all?
I haven't looked for many a year at things upon the floor
If I sort them all out, I can make room for more

I remember having that book 'for merit in class two'
Someone else chose it, and I never read it through
As I did not like history -it always made me sad
Hard times, all those wars, people cruel and so bad

That tennis racquet, I recall, was a favourite of mine
Rather too heavy - but seemed brilliant at the time
I loved to play, not good or skilled, but I was very keen
Out of doors and active my happiest days have been

That jumper has many holes, the moths have had a party
Warm it was in winter cold, but itchy and so scratchy
I knitted it with pride, the wool, coarse - yet colour fine
But when I later wore it, I regretted every line

I remember playing with that rag doll upon the floor
It has lost an arm and leg, it couldn't lose much more
It was the only doll I ever had, I think I  love it still
It was a comfort when I was small and often very ill

Did I really paint the picture, by that old white chair?
Goodness me. What a mess, I wonder that I dare
I never was an artist, designs - a total blur to me
I would try very hard, but paint nothing fit to see

The monopoly is still in its box. Why did I never win?
What trouble we used to cause when we made such a din
Do I need these memories ? Which of them should I keep?
Or should I just decide to pile them in a heap?

Into a sack these items place, put in this room some light
Use it for some purpose new and paint it all so bright
Life is to be lived now, each moment every day
I don't need this clutter, I'll throw all these things away

# Contrast

Picture these two different scenes
Decide which seems the best
Which one would be like you?
Am I different from all the rest?

I went for a walk one day
By water that was so calm
The sun many reflections made
No wind, the air was warm
A perfect place, you would think
To enjoy an hour or two
But some children were intent
On creating a loud 'to do'
Shouting and screaming loud
With each other they did fight
So I kept on walking
Away from the sound and sight

On the water, that was so calm
Two ducks were swimming by
With six ducklings side by side
No noise, no fuss, no cry
They swam together easily
Without any fighting seen
A beautiful example shown
To those children who had been
Shouting and screaming loud
With each other they did fight
So I stayed and I watched
The beautiful sound and sight

# Clouds Of Love

The little boy was playing
In his garden with a ball
He fell down with a bump
But he didn't cry at all

From there he saw the sky above
And then he laughed and said
'Can you see that field of clouds?
It is just above my head

They are playing a game of chase
As they run across the sky
I wish that I could join them
Can I? If I really, really try?'

He skipped around and he jumped
And held his hands up high
'Maybe when I grow big and tall'

**That game money couldn't buy**

# Aunt Polly's Gift

Growing up in wartime there was but little joy
For children in the country who barely had a toy
I was nearly seven years old, when Aunt Polly gave to me
A tea service, in a box – to make a dolly's tea
Four cups, five saucers , but no plates for any cake
Sugar bowl, jug and teapot, a lovely sight did make
Made of plain white china with a fluted rim of gold
'Be very, very careful', imaginary friends were told

Memories of childhood are stored deep in my mind
It is the only toy still left, at least that I can find
Aunt Polly worked very hard, but clearly, I could see
In choosing her 'leaving' gift, **she** had thought of me
That meant such a lot, probably more than any knew
Illness dogged my childhood and happy days were few
I didn't 'jump 'in puddles, run around in winter's snow
Normal things that children do, I usually couldn't know

That lovely gift gave me the chance, alone, to play a game
Time was more bearable, when all days seemed the same
I wonder if she ever knew the service that she did?
That gift helped me to cope, when a future was well hid
It let me know that someone else realised I was there
And that they thought of me, maybe said a little prayer
'God, please see how good and brave she tries to be'
 I simply thought -
                    'something special **now** belongs to me'

# The Birth Day Cake.

'In my family I do not think that I am loved so dearly
As my brother, no, not as much, no, not even nearly
No one ever shouts at him, never cross with him, just me
We both get pocket money, but he gets more, I see
He is called a good boy, and that can make me sad
As when I have 'my tantrums', I feel I must be bad
I know I scream and shout a lot, make everyone so cross
It's only because I cannot get my message clear across
I want to be the same as him, to do what he can do
I want to be loved as much. Oh, why can't it be true?'

'My little girl, you must learn, all are special in many ways
Listen to what I say to you, and remember it all your days
When any little child is born, each has a birth-day cake
Though they all look different, the same things are used to make
Each one is made with great love and prepared with tender care
Another does not take a slice, your cake no one can share
Each cake is worth the same, no cake heavier than another
The only difference is outside, pink -a girl, blue -a brother
So understand that you **are** loved, you are so very dear
But he arrived before you came, you were not even here

Your parents knew him first, but **he** shares them with you
He hasn't to mind at all – lots of things for you he'll do
Yes, you do make more noise – it's just that's how you are
You are delightful, full of fun, no one could love you more
He has had his younger years, he has had the early nights
He has grown well past that time, he now has 'older rights'
Stop thinking that he has your cake – it's not for him at all
But neither can you have **his** cake, into **your** hands it will not fall
If you understand this now, then much happier you will be
You will always be loved the same -
                            by your parents and by me'